Camera
ON THE
CLYDE

Published by:

Ferry Publications, PO Box 33,
Ramsey, Isle of Man IM99 4LP

Tel: +44 (0) 1624 898446 Fax: +44 (0) 1624 898449

E-mail: ferrypubs@manx.net
Website: www.ferrypubs.co.uk

FERRY
Publications

Ann Glen and Bruce Peter

CAMERA ON THE CLYDE
Foreword

For nearly all of his long life, A. Ernest Glen was a ship enthusiast. Indeed, his interests were wide-ranging, encompassing transport, engineering, history and archaeology. Born into a well-to-do Victorian household in the West End of Glasgow in 1896, he was given his first camera, a Box Brownie, when aged only twelve.

His father had built up a grocery business in the city - he was one of the early entrepreneurs who realised that buying in bulk and selling through multiple outlets was advantageous. He worked hard and prospered to such an extent that he was able to retire early.

Ernest first sailed from Glasgow on the upper stretches of the Clyde aboard the Cluthas, little ferries that plied up and down the river - hence they were given the Latin version of its name. At that time the Clyde was at its peak as a port with great numbers of steamers and large sailing ships tied along its quay walls, in its docks and at buoys in the centre of the channel. When he asked his parents about the numerous floating objects which marred its surface he was told to 'hold his tongue' - adequate sewage works had yet to be constructed and the river was foul.

In the 1900s the Glens went on holiday to Whiting Bay on Arran and Rothesay - to the latter at Easter as it was far too crowded in the summer. Gourock was another favourite place as a rented flat there had a big bow window where a retired ship's captain had thoughtfully installed a telescope giving a superb view of the Firth and its shipping. It was here that Ernest's passion for ships first emerged - the many types of vessel from puffers to ocean liners that could be seen were a constant source of fascination to a boy; he learned to distinguish the shipping lines and could soon tell their vessels from the funnel colours and the characteristic outlines they had. To add to the bustle, there were also the rival fleets of Clyde steamers - numbering over forty in the summer months - racing to and from the piers which were numerous both on the river and the Firth.

Surprisingly, most of Ernest's early shipping knowledge came from his mother, Anne Marshall, whose brother was a port doctor in Glasgow and an expert on tropical diseases. When a ship lay at the Tail of the Bank with the yellow flag hoisted, it was probable that Uncle George would be summoned on board. She was well acquainted with the shipping families and was a friend of the Williamsons, the steamer owners. Ernest's first home was at Partickhill where in summer his mother could check the time on her kitchen clock by the passage of the noble MacBrayne steamer *Columba* making her daily journey down river - the ship left the Broomielaw at 7.10am - and he might be held up at the window to see her sweep by.

The acquisition of that simple camera began a life-long enthusiasm for photography, especially of ships and railways. When his first film came to be processed in the family's kitchen, Ernest's mother was just as excited as he was. Ever eager to help, she washed the film under the hot tap and was horrified to see the images disappear down the sink as so much jelly. Subsequent films and glass plates were successfully processed, and amongst his early photographs of shipping are images of the Cunarder *Aquitania* under construction at John Brown's shipyard. At Glasgow Academy where he went to school, the Art Master set up a Photographic Society with competitions and excursions in which Ernest took part.

*Being a teetotal steamer, the **Ivanhoe** was a favourite with Ernest's mother. Built in 1880 for the Frith of Clyde Steam Packet Company (sic), she was popular on the Arran route. Here the steamer blackens the skies as she leaves Brodick about 1908.*

*While the **Ivanhoe** was in the ownership of the CSP, these discerning middle-class passengers were enjoying a summer sail to Arran, the steamer going out by the Kyles of Bute and back by Garroch Head – a very popular excursion.*

In 1914 Ernest went to Glasgow University to study mechanical engineering but, tragically for him, the First World War intervened and he served in the Cameronians (Scottish Rifles), a Lowland regiment. He was sent to the trenches of France where, at Arras in December 1917, he was blown up and buried alive. He owed his survival to his protective tin hat and to those who dug him out.

When recovering in hospital from injuries and shell-shock, first in London and then at Craiglockhart in Edinburgh, a 21st birthday present was a reflex camera. It took excellent photos on glass quarter plates but had a delicate mechanism dependent on elastic bands which gave out all too soon. By the mid-1920s, however, a more reliable camera with a high-quality Zeiss Tessar lens was obtained and some of Ernest's best photographs were taken with it.

A remarkable opportunity came his way around this time. With a university degree in engineering and practical experience under his belt, gained by working with the Caledonian Railway at its St. Rollox Works, he chose to expand his knowledge of civil engineering. So, in 1926, he was appointed to the Clyde

Navigation Trust (CNT) where his first assignment was as a resident engineer during the building of King George V Dock or 'KGV' as it became known. At that time, this dock was the biggest in Scotland. When Ernest first went to the site near Shieldhall, the ground was part of a farm and he began marking off and setting out the dock in what had been a barley field. The great enterprise was meant to be the first of a series of such docks on the Clyde, but trade depression and war intervened - no others were ever constructed.

The site at King George V Dock was well positioned for a grandstand view of the Clyde and the shipping that sailed on its waters, but also strategically located for the launching of vessels. On the north bank, a line-up of shipyards stretched from Barclay Curle's Clydeholm yard, via Connell's yard, Mechan's works, Harland & Wolff's engine works, through Blythswood's and Yarrow's, to Barclay Curle's Elderslie dockyard. In fact, the outlook from KGV could be said to embrace the whole gamut of marine engineering. In 1927, over 600,000 tons of new shipping was Clyde-built and it was one of the periods of greatest ever activity

*By 1935 the **Duchess of Argyll** was cruising alternately between Gourock and Campbeltown or Inveraray. Her elegance is emphasised in an evening view taken at Dunoon.*

on the river. These were years when one-fifth of the world's shipping was launched in and around Glasgow. The riversides reverberated with the clamour of riveting and the ring of hammers on steel. The banks were so packed with shipyards that rights of way for those on foot had to be maintained on shaky staging round the sterns of vessels under construction.

Being a Clyde Trust man was naturally a passport to travelling on the cross-river ferries or exploring the docks. The CNT was known as the 'Hielan'man's Navy' because so many Gaelic speakers and natives of the West Coast were employed in it. So Kingston Dock, General Terminus and Lancefield Quays, Stobcross and Plantation Quays, Yorkhill, Prince's and Queen's Docks and many more began to figure as venues in his meticulous photographic records - and of course the Broomielaw itself. Ernest was also knowledgeable about the engineering feats which had made the Clyde into a navigable river - from John Golbourne's efforts in the

*Here the **Duchess of Montrose** is seen in Cardwell Bay at Gourock in 1931.*

*The **Duchess of Fife**, viewed off Craigmore in the early 1930s, shows the open bridge with canvas 'dodgers', so typical of the older steamers, and the exposed forward portion of the saloon deck relished by some passengers.*

18th century using the stream and tidal scour to deepen the channel to the formation of the Lang Dyke and the blasting away of such obstructions as the troublesome Elderslie Rock. The construction of KGV taught him much about the fickle bed of the river with its dour clays and treacherous running sands. He used to describe the Clyde as a 'canal without locks'.

Ernest had a particular affection for Clyde steamers and a solid knowledge of them too. He liked to recount the days of boyhood rivalries when the merits of the Caledonian Steam Packet Company's elegant *Duchess of Argyll* (a pioneering turbine ship) versus the Glasgow & South Western Railway's paddle steamer *Glen Sannox* were hotly debated. He never cared much for the latter, having been seasick on board many years previously while on a stormy crossing to Arran with his mother.

Some of the Clyde steamers of the pre-First World War era were the last word in *fin de siècle* elegance. Those of the Caledonian Steam Packet Company (CSP), for example, had white boot-topping, dark blue hulls with gold lining and scrollwork ornamentation, pale pink saloon deck window surrounds, varnished teak deckhouses and buff funnels. With their fine hull lines and graceful counter sterns, these vessels - and those of the other pre-grouping Clyde fleets - made a tremendous impression on young Ernest. Indeed, their speed, style and fine craftsmanship reflected Glasgow's design and engineering expertise when the city was at the height of its industrial power.

However, there was a downside - the smoke which they produced. It was black and frequently there was plenty of it, especially if vessels were racing. This was an activity in which captains of rival steamer companies were prone to indulge. Coal was cheap and so was the labour in the stokeholds. The result was that soot floated on the waters of the Firth, staining its shores, and captains could only be fined if their ship was making smoke when tied up at a pier.

For Ernest, the scrapping of MacBrayne's magnificent *Columba* in 1936 and the commissioning of a series of new and squat motor vessels - the *Lochmor*, *Lochearn* and *Lochfyne* - signalled the beginning of the end of an era. For his journeys, he much preferred the Caledonian Steam Packet (LMS) turbine steamers *Duchess of Hamilton* and *Duchess of Montrose* which gave a smoother, quieter

*The **Duchess of Montrose** is dressed overall at Gourock in 1949 as she is prepared for an excursion round Arran for the Clyde River Steamer Club.*

*Designed for the relaxed itineraries of lochside piers, the **Marchioness of Lorne** was very new when approaching Gourock in the summer of 1935.*

passage and retained the lofty funnels and elegant proportions of their Edwardian predecessors. The newest 'Caley' paddle steamers, *Jupiter*, *Juno*, *Caledonia* and *Marchioness of Lorne*, were less well liked as these were designed without any paddle-box embellishments so as to look more like turbine ships, which many steamer enthusiasts thought was just deception.

In the 1930s, with so many old boyhood favourites being withdrawn and First War losses replaced, the Clyde River Steamer Club (CRSC) was established and Ernest was a founder member. These years saw the peak of his photography with a progression of

Craigendoran with its extensive railway installations and steamer pier had been the North British Railway's gateway to the Clyde coast. Taking a train from Glasgow's Queen Street or Charing Cross west along the shores of the Firth of Clyde brought mounting excitement approaching Craigendoran – which steamers would be waiting there? Here in BR years the **Jeanie Deans** *and the* **Waverley** *are in view.*

film types being used - Pathé, Ensign Speedy and Wellington were superseded by Agfa Isochrome and Kodak Verichrome. He noted the exposure and aperture used for every photograph taken. Memorable excursions with his friend Ronald McKim, or his wife Isobel, either to the by-waters of the Firth or to special steamer events, were captured. Films were developed and printed at home in a dark room, just a modified cupboard in the basement of his house. Ernest's skill as a photographer in composing photographs with a fixed lens camera was always praised.

The Second World War put a temporary stop to photography. Ronald McKim was hauled in by Naval Intelligence for appearing to take a photo from Kirn Pier of vessels at the Tail of the Bank - there was some embarrassment in Admiralty circles when he produced his Special Constable's police identification and demonstrated that he was only filling his pipe! Yet it was still possible to go ship-spotting. Tram trips out to Yoker and a brisk walk to the riverside led past the old power station to the Renfrew Ferry. This clanked across on chains and was of course steam-powered. There were always hopes that a freighter or a troopship would be inward- or outward-bound, holding up the ferry's passage and thereby allowing close-up viewing. However, the distinctive colours of pre-war had been painted over in grey and even

Laid up in the Albert Harbour at Greenock on 16 April 1954 are, from left to right, **Ashton, Countess of Breadalbane** *and* **Marchioness of Graham.** *This basin was a regular place for over-wintering CSP vessels while awaiting service in the summer months. In the distance can be seen* **Ardyne, Glen Sannox** *and* **Lairds Isle.**

merchantmen bristled with guns.

Once on the south bank, a rare line-up of elderly vessels was to be seen in Renfrew Harbour - known to some as the Pudzeoch Basin on account of a long-lost burn - where the Clyde Trust kept elderly replacements for their ferries at Erskine and Renfrew. Quite apart from the CNT presence and the seediness of this little dock, the strange vessels and the assortment of nautical paraphernalia it held were intriguing.

Another ploy was to go to Merkland Street by subway to

embark on the Meadowside Ferry, one of the small maroon-painted CNT vessels which chugged across the river before bumping into the landing stages and appearing partially to climb up the steps. At busy times, these ferries swarmed with shipyard workers with their 'bunnets' and often filthy dungarees smelling of 'biled ile' (boiled oil) and sweat. After a stroll through tenement streets past the gates of shipyards and engine works, the tour would be completed with a return trip on the Kelvinhaugh Ferry before heading back from Govan by subway. Near Harland & Wolff's yard

at weekends, a flotilla of the little ferries would be lined up on the riverside with funnels tipped back and wisps of smoke issuing from within.

By 1945 there had been more losses and the few steamers which had maintained essential Clyde services had become war-weary. The first post-war sailing was to Rothesay on the *Lucy Ashton*, still in grey paint and treading a careful path through the boom, a massive net which stretched from Dunoon to the Cloch. It was a defence against submarines entering the anchorage at the Tail of the Bank where convoys were assembled.

Colour returned when the steamers reverted to their former liveries and there was a newcomer to explore - the *Waverley*, the fourth with that name and now the last seagoing paddle steamer in the world. Reviews of the Fleet, commemorative sailings, steamer anniversaries - such as round Arran on the *Duchess of Montrose* - and cruises were again to be enjoyed. An annual outing was to Ardrossan with Graham Langmuir, another doyen of the CRSC, to see the Isle of Man boats. Once again, there were the trips from Bridge Wharf on the *Queen Mary II* to Rothesay and the Kyles of Bute or on the *Duchess of Hamilton* to Campbeltown. En route to Gourock, abandoned piers such as Govan and Partick would be pointed out. As the steamer slid past KGV, Ernest would gaze at the great concrete 'bull noses' that formed the mouth of the dock. "These are my monuments", he would say, "it took me six weeks of hard work to do the calculations for them."

In spring there were lengthy plods round the Albert Harbour at Greenock to view the assortment of shipping there or to slipways to see old favourites hauled out for such routine jobs as having plating replaced or their 'bottoms scraped'. In early summer, a train might be caught at Charing Cross or Anniesland to go to Craigendoran. With the train pounding west along the coast, who would be first to catch sight of the steamers alongside the pier there? Was it the *Jeanie Deans* ? Or the *Talisman*? Sometimes there was a departure from Central Station bound for Gourock to have a sail on the *Jupiter* to Dunoon or Rothesay, or to travel further west to Wemyss Bay boarding the 'Wee Fife', as the veteran paddle steamer *Duchess of Fife* was fondly known.

Although black and white photography was never entirely given up, a second-hand 35mm camera purchased in 1951 allowed colour to be captured when the Clyde was still a busy river. In fact Ernest's first post-war colour slides were taken at Oban during the May Holiday - showing some of MacBrayne's little motor ships and their elegant turbine excursion steamer *King George V*.

Gradually, however, the glories departed; the shipyards - which had numbered 18 in 1954 - were rapidly reduced until today there are only three. It was depressing for someone who had known the Clyde in its heyday when the docks had swarmed with ships. Even so, Ernest continued to follow shipping activities on the river and the Firth - he went to the launch of Caledonian MacBrayne's *Isle of Arran* in December 1983 when he was approaching ninety years of age. He reckoned that this was some achievement for a 'wreck from the First World War', as he described himself. Since the latter 1930s, he had not been able to hold down a regular job and now, with only limited means, photography was becoming a luxury. A kenspeckle figure in plus-fours and raincoat or sometimes wearing a kilt, he liked to capture the changing scene on the river, methodically keeping records of his films in notebooks. He was an acknowledged expert and arbiter to whom others deferred - 'Ernest will know' - and he found happiness and solace among friends who shared his interest and enthusiasm for the ships and steamers of the Clyde and Western Isles. We hope that this album of Ernest's photographs, taken on these waters, will also give similar pleasure.

Ann Glen and Bruce Peter
September 2009

The **Marchioness of Graham**, *built by Fairfields in 1936, was a modern turbine steamer as this view taken at Ardrossan on 16 July 1937 shows. Placed on the demanding Ardrossan–Arran route, her promenade deck was designed for vehicle transport as car traffic to and from the island was increasing, but it could also accommodate penned livestock.*

The smart **Duchess of Montrose (I)** was launched from the yard of John Brown & Co Ltd at Clydebank in 1902 for the CSP. Smaller in size than the **Duchess of Rothesay**, and with a trial speed of only 16 knots, she was no flyer. Based at Ayr for excursion work, she also served on other routes and is seen leaving Rothesay in May 1914. Taken over by the Admiralty in the First World War, the **Duchess of Montrose** was mined off the Belgian coast in 1917.

The Caledonian Steam Packet Company began modestly in 1888 by purchasing two steamers. The **Madge Wildfire**, built in Ayr two years previously, was one. Here in a photograph taken by Ernest Glen when a schoolboy, she leaves Gourock in April 1908 when on the Kilcreggan, Cove and Blairmore run.

The **Edinburgh Castle** was an old steamer built at Port Glasgow in 1879 for the Lochgoil & Lochlong Steamboat Company. Here showing her exceptionally large paddle-boxes, she splashes away from Gourock in April 1909. By this time, as a teenager, Ernest Glen had a quarter-plate camera.

The **Eagle III** *was launched for the Buchanan fleet in 1910 and unusually the numeral was part of the steamer's name. Built on sub-contract from A & J Inglis, she suffered instability but alterations were made enabling her to sail satisfactorily. Here in Buchanan Steamers' livery, she approaches Renfrew Wharf in June 1914.*

*In the 1900s the handiness and economy of paddle steamers resulted in new orders being placed for such ships. The **Queen-Empress** was constructed at Port Glasgow in 1912 for the Williamson fleet and served on up river runs. In June 1914 she was viewed leaving Renfrew Pier.*

*A view from June 1914 shows the **Ivanhoe** displaying white funnels with black tops and black paddle-boxes, the style of her new owners, Turbine Steamers Ltd, as she passes up river at Erskine Ferry. She was withdrawn in 1920.*

*When the **King Edward** was launched at Wm Denny's yard at Dumbarton in 1901, she was the world's first passenger ship to be driven by steam turbines. She is seen at Greenock's Albert Harbour in September 1921.*

*The **Duchess of Fife**, designed by Percy A. Hillhouse who became Professor of Naval Architecture at Glasgow University, was launched by Fairfields at Govan in 1903. Here, she swings away from Rothesay in May 1922.*

*A steamer of the Clyde's 'golden age' was the **Duchess of Rothesay**. Launched at Clydebank in 1895, her smart looks were widely acclaimed. She had the title 'cock of the walk' and for a time carried a small weathercock on her masthead. The 'Duchess' sailed on various routes for the CSP, mainly to Rothesay from Gourock or Wemyss Bay but also further afield.*

*The **Juno** (I) enters Troon Harbour in September 1922 . Built in 1898, she was described as 'big, beamy and beautiful'. Although designed for the English Channel coast, the G&SWR bought her before completion. Averaging 19 knots on trials guaranteed her popularity as the Ayr excursion steamer but she also proved a sturdy ship in rough waters.*

*In 1892 the paddle steamer **Glen Sannox** (1) was built at Clydebank for the Glasgow & South Western Railway Company. One of the most impressive vessels on the Firth, she was a worthy competitor for the other fleets. On trials, the **Glen Sannox** attained a speed of over 19 knots. In September 1922 with winter boarding in place, she was photographed passing Winton Pier at Ardrossan.*

*The Glasgow & South Western Railway's **Jupiter** (I) calls at Greenock for coaling in September 1921 - sailing ship masts are visible in the background. Built by J & G Thomson at Clydebank in 1896, this steamer served on the Arran via the Kyles of Bute run in pre-First World War days. She was a minesweeper during that conflict and after overhaul was used on a variety of excursions until withdrawn and broken up at Barrow in 1935.*

*Formerly a G&SWR steamer, the **Mercury** (I) was delivered by Napier, Shanks & Bell at Yoker in 1892. She proved a fast and therefore attractive ship on the Kyles of Bute route. Here, she is seen off Dunoon in May 1922. After the 1933 season she was laid up and sold for scrapping.*

*In Williamson-Buchanan colours, the **Eagle III** prepares to call at Frisky Pier at Bowling Harbour on 20 June 1923. As a Williamson-Buchanan steamer, she typically cruised down river from Glasgow on the forenoon run to Rothesay but also took other excursions in the holiday months.*

Although ordered for the Williamson fleet, the **Kylemore** began her sailing days in 1897 as a steamer at Eastbourne. In 1904 she came to the Clyde for Williamson but was shortly sold to the G&SWR, sailing as the Vulcan. Within four years she was back with Williamson as the **Kylemore**. These views, taken from the Water's Neb by the Clyde, show the **Kylemore** sweeping past Rothesay Dock on the afternoon run from Glasgow to Rothesay on 2 June 1923. John Brown's Clydebank yard is in the background.

By 19 August 1923, the **Duchess of Rothesay** *has had her funnel repainted with the red band of the LMS livery, a scheme known as 'bumbee tartan.' Here, she makes a rousing departure from Innellan.*

Launched in 1899, the **Waverley (III)** *was larger than any previous steamer in the North British fleet. On trials her speed was in excess of 19 knots, placing her among the swiftest of the Clyde paddle steamers.*

The **Atalanta** *was the first and only turbine steamer in the Glasgow & South Western Railway fleet, coming from John Brown & Company at Clydebank in 1906. Here she is moored at Gourock on 28 June 1923. Following the railway groupings, she is sporting the 'bumbee tartan' funnel of the London, Midland & Scottish Railway.*

The **Marchioness of Breadalbane**, *built at Port Glasgow, entered the CSP fleet in 1890. She was stationed at Wemyss Bay – one of the Clyde's most exposed piers – as an all-year-round steamer on the Rothesay run and stories tell of her battling successfully through the gales. After service as a minesweeper in the First World War, the* **Marchioness of Breadalbane** *became well known as the Millport steamer. Here she is off Gourock in 1923 in LMS colours including a 'bumbee tartan' funnel.*

Built in 1878 for David Hutcheson & Company, the **Columba (I)** *is acknowledged as 'the finest and most famous steamer that ever sailed on the Clyde'. She became a MacBrayne ship the following year. For over fifty years, the* **Columba** *maintained the passenger and mail service on the 'Royal Route' from Glasgow to Ardrishaig in summer. Here, she is seen on the Firth of Clyde on 10 May 1923.*

*On 10 August 1923, the **Columba** is captured racing towards Innellan where daily calls were made.*

*Three MacBrayne steamers lie in Bowling Harbour in the winter of 1924. Nearest the camera is the **Columba** of 1878 with the **Chevalier** (II) of 1866 and the **Mountaineer** (III) of 1910 alongside. Summer season steamers were laid up in the winter months in sheltered confines where they awaited annual overhaul before their busy cruise schedules on the Firth of Clyde and in the West Highlands.*

*On 10 September 1932, the **Columba** is moored at Tarbert on Loch Fyne. There were devotees for whom sailing on the Clyde meant only one steamer – the **Columba**. To their regret, she was withdrawn in 1935 and was broken up at Dalmuir.*

*In July 1933 MacBrayne's **Fusilier** is seen powering away from Broadford on the Isle of Skye. Built in 1888 at Paisley, she was sold for further work in 1934, becoming the **Lady Orme** on the North Wales coast, and as the **Crestawave**, was broken up in 1938.*

*Here in July 1923, the **Fusilier** is seen alongside the old pier with its railway lines at Fort William. At this date the steamer was often based at Oban in summer and was laid up in winter.*

*On 1 July 1933 the **Fusilier** was photographed approaching the pier at Portree when serving ports on the Isle of Skye.*

The steamer **Fusilier** *at anchor in the rugged setting of Loch Scavaig in July 1933. MacBraynes stationed a boat here in summer to take passengers ashore to vi*
Loch Coruisk and the Cuillins.

For thirty years the little steamer **Pioneer** *(III) maintained the route between Islay, Jura and West Loch Tarbert for MacBraynes. She came from the Inglis yard in 1905 and had very small paddle wheels to take account of the shallow waters of the loch. She is seen there on 10 September 1932 with planks for loading motor vehicles in place. Looking on is Ernest Glen's wife Isobel seated beside his car, a Morris Oxford coupé of 1927, now preserved in a motor museum.*

*Built in 1908 for the MacBrayne fleet, the **Lochinvar** was a pioneering motor ship initially having paraffin engines, which reputedly could be heard before she was seen. Here the Lochinvar is at Oban with Kerrera as a backdrop in the summer of 1924.*

*The **Glencoe** was built for Sir James Matheson of Stornoway in 1846 and first named **Mary Jane** after his wife. Here on show at the Broomielaw on 4 June 1931 during Glasgow's Civic Week, she was the oldest steamer in the MacBrayne fleet and is alongside the diesel-electric **Lochfyne**, the newest vessel.*

*The second **Lord of the Isles** came from the yard of D & W Henderson in 1891 for service with the Glasgow & Inveraray Steamboat Company. The new steamer was spacious, had a good turn of speed and soon became a rival for MacBrayne's RMS **Columba**. Competition from the new turbine steamers relegated the **Lord of the Isles** to excursions from Glasgow; here the steamer is approaching Gourock Pier on 28 May 1927.*

*The first turbine steamer to be ordered for the CSP fleet was the elegant **Duchess of Argyll**, built by Wm Denny of Dumbarton in 1906. On 28 August 1931 in LMS colours, the steamer is seen in Gourock Bay.*

*The **King George V** was delivered to Turbine Steamers Ltd in 1926. She is shown arriving at Gourock in May 1927.*

*Sailing on the open Ardrossan–Arran route earned the **Atalanta**, which had fine lines as this bow shot from September 1928 shows, a name for poor seakeeping qualities.*

*Caught in evening sunlight, the **King George V** is shown arriving at Gourock on 15 August 1930. Following re-boilering, her funnels now have naval tops.*

*The **Glen Sannox** (II), built by Wm Denny at Dumbarton, was a turbine vessel which replaced the paddle steamer of the same name on the Arran run in 1925. She is seen first in a calm Brodick Bay in the latter 1920s.*

The King George V *at Inveraray Pier on 7 September 1929.*

*The **Waverley** (III), now in the London & North Eastern Railway fleet, is seen off Innellan in the early 1930s.*

*The **Lucy Ashton** was launched at Rutherglen in 1888 for the North British Steam Packet Company and was placed on the Holy Loch run. Here she is seen in LNER livery sailing past the Esplanade at Gourock on 21 September 1932.*

*Ordered by the North British Railway, the **Marmion** came from the yard of A & J Inglis Ltd in 1906. Here the **Marmion** is seen swinging towards Rothesay Pier on 13 August 1931 with ships laid up on account of the trade depression in the background.*

*Here the **Mercury (I)** is seen coming into Gourock in breezy weather on 28 August 1931 when in LMS colours. Formerly a G&SWR steamer, she was built at Yoker in 1892 and soon proved a fast and therefore attractive ship on the Kyles of Bute route. The **Mercury's** First World War adventures as a minesweeper were remarkable. She first had her stern blown off and no sooner was she back in service than her bow was sheared off by a mine. After the 1933 season she was laid up and sold for scrapping.*

*A stormy passage off Ardrossan in the mid-1930s sees the **Glen Sannox** rolling and pitching uncomfortably as she makes for that harbour.*

*On 13 June 1931 the **Duchess of Rothesay** shows her classic lines as she swings towards Princes Pier at Greenock.*

The **Caledonia** (I) *was constructed at Port Glasgow for the Caledonian Steam Packet Company in 1889 – the first Clyde vessel built for that fleet and the first with compound machinery. Initially, the* **Caledonia** *took the Rothesay run but was to become closely associated with the Holy Loch route from Gourock. Here the* **Caledonia** *comes into Gourock on a blustery day in August 1931 when in LMS colours. In 1933 she was withdrawn and broken up at Barrow.*

The **Duchess of Montrose** (II) *was launched by Wm Denny of Dumbarton in 1930. As the first 'one class' ship on the Clyde, her interiors were a novelty. Her excursions 'Round Arran' and to Ailsa Craig took on the character of mini-cruises on a comfortable ship. Here the* **Duchess of Montrose** *is seen in Cardwell Bay at Gourock in 1931.*

The Loch Lomond steamers were the joint responsibility of two railway companies, the Caledonian and North British. When the design of the **Prince George** *was disputed, it went the length of arbitration. Built by A & J Inglis and launched in 1898 on the Clyde, delivery was via the River Leven to Balloch. The* **Prince George** *was on the summer service calling at all piers to Ardlui where she is seen on 21 September 1929, with Ernest's wife, Isobel, looking on.*

The **Prince Edward** *was launched in 1911 and was larger than other Loch Lomond steamers. Here she leaves Ardlui at the head of Loch Lomond on 8 August 1936.*

The **Princess May** *began her career on Loch Lomond in 1899 after being launched from the Inglis yard on the Clyde. On 1 June 1932 the neglected steamer was at anchor in Drumkinnon Bay.*

In 1933 the handsome turbine steamer **Queen Mary** came from Wm Denny of Dumbarton. She joined the fleet of Williamson-Buchanan and, being well appointed, won much custom. At 1,014 gross registered tons, she was the largest ever Clyde steamer. In anticipation of the completion of the Cunard liner **Queen Mary** at Clydebank, the Clyde steamer's name was changed to **Queen Mary II**. Here, she is seen off Dunoon Pier on 10 August 1939.

The **Queen Mary** *is seen leaving Rothesay on 8 June 1933 when very new.*

The **Marchioness of Breadalbane** *comes into Princes Pier at Greenock on 23 August 1934. Sold to shipbreakers in 1935, she actually saw further use as an excursion steamer on the east coast of England for two years.*

The **Glen Rosa** *was a G&SWR steamer built by J & G Thomson Ltd at Clydebank in 1893 and was generally on the run from Fairlie to Rothesay via Millport and Kilchattan Bay. In the winter season, she was the regular steamer on the stormy Ardrossan–Arran route – hence her extra-stout construction. Here the* **Glen Rosa***, in LMS livery, is seen leaving Largs in boisterous weather on 27 July 1934.*

The **Glen Sannox** *rests at Ardrossan's Winton Pier on 18 June 1934.*

During the Glasgow Fair Holiday of 1934, the **Atalanta** *is seen at a choppy Ardrossan Harbour with the Isle of Man Steam Packet Company turbine steamer* **Mona's Queen**. *Latterly, the* **Atalanta** *took up the Wemyss Bay–Millport run.*

*The **Glen Sannox** (II) leaves Ardrossan Harbour in fine style on 27 July 1934. Her regular sailings were from Ardrossan to Brodick and also to Campbeltown.*

The Mercury (II) came from Fairfields, joining the LMS Clyde fleet in 1934. Here, she is seen at Gourock on 23 August that year.

The **Mercury** *was on Kyles of Bute cruises from Greenock and Gourock. She is also seen at Princes Pier in Greenock when very new in 1934.*

The new generation of CSP steamers had enclosed paddle-boxes, which gave the impression of turbine ships, as the side view of the **Mercury** *and the* **Marchioness of Lorne,** *taken off Gourock on 13 June 1935, shows. While on war service in 1940, the* **Mercury** *was damaged by a mine and sank while on tow in the Irish Sea.*

A view from 29 August 1936 sees the **King Edward** *making plenty of smoke in Rothesay Bay. During the Second World War, the steamer was a tender in the Firth of Clyde but post-war returned to a forenoon excursion from Glasgow to Rothesay and the Kyles of Bute. In 1952 this revolutionary ship was sold for scrapping, one of the turbines only being preserved.*

With her distinctive Williamson-Buchanan white funnel, the *Kylemore* is also seen dashing away from Gourock on 13 June 1936 when packed with passengers on a Glasgow Saturday excursion.

The motor launch **Wee Cumbrae** was built by *Wm Denny* at *Dumbarton* to supplement the ferry service between Largs and Millport. She began sailing in 1935 but could only carry 60 passengers in her saloons. This view from 29 August 1936 shows the **Wee Cumbrae** dwarfed by Largs Pier which is thronged with holidaymakers.

The **Queen Alexandra (II)** was delivered to Turbine Steamers Ltd from Denny's yard at Dumbarton in 1912. She is seen approaching Princes Pier, Greenock on 13 June 1935.

MacBrayne's Lochnevis, *dating from 1934, was a diesel-electric vessel launched by Wm Denny at Dumbarton. While chubby in appearance and noisy, improvements had been made in reducing vibration. Designed for year-round 'day use' on the Mallaig, Kyle and Portree mail service, the ship was well appointed. On 3 August 1935, the* Lochnevis *is viewed approaching and leaving Mallaig. She was withdrawn in 1969.*

The Iona (III) was well known and widely admired. Launched in 1864 for David Hutcheson, she acquired the lavish fittings and furnishings of a steamer of the same name sold for blockade running in the American Civil War. The Iona was first on the Ardrishaig route to Glasgow and by 1879 was MacBrayne-owned. Viewed on Loch Linnhe on 5 August 1935, the Iona was on the Oban-Fort William run but was shortly withdrawn and scrapped the following year.

Here MacBrayne's Gondolier is seen laid up for the winter at Foyers Pier on Loch Ness on 10 September 1935. A favourite with the travelling public, the Gondolier was withdrawn and scrapped early in the Second World War.

This steamer, built in 1896 at Port Glasgow, was first the Laird Line ship **Lily.** *After transfer to Burns & Laird in 1922 she was renamed the* **Lairdspool** *in 1929 and was in the Irish trade. In 1937 she entered MacBrayne's fleet with the name* **Lochgorm,** *and was placed on the cargo service from Glasgow to Stornoway. She is seen at Lancefield Quay on 15 August 1938. The* **Lochgorm** *was withdrawn in 1951.*

The **Lochgarry** *was a screw steamer built in 1898 by A & J Inglis for the Ardrossan Shipping Company and launched as the* **Vulture.** *By 1936 as a Coast Lines ship with the better name of* **Lairdsrock,** *she became part of the MacBrayne fleet. After an extensive refit, she was engaged on Western Isles cruises and was well known on the Stornoway run. In 1942 she was wrecked off the Irish coast.*

*The **Loch Aline** was originally MacBrayne's **Plover** (II), a screw steamer built in 1904 at Bowling. Placed on Hebridean services, she performed well. In 1934 the ship was transformed with a buff funnel and white bulwarks at Ardrossan for the MacBrayne Directors' summer use. She was there on 30 September 1935 along with the **Lairds Isle**, the latter sporting the new Burns & Laird blue band on her funnels.*

*The **Dalriada**, launched at Port Glasgow in 1926 for the Campbeltown & Glasgow Steam Packet Joint Stock Co Ltd – a business with a long name and a long history - sailed on the lengthy Glasgow to Campbeltown route, a popular 'out and back' day tour. She was dwarfed by a very large funnel – for economical natural draught in winter – but in summer forced draught could produce over 17 knots. The Dalriada was reputed to be the fastest single-screw steamship in the world.*

*Here, the LNER steamer **Marmion** approaches Craigendoran on 15 June 1935. By then, her accommodation had been improved for passenger comfort with a lounge and tea-room replacing her plain saloon.*

The **Kenilworth** *joined the North British fleet in 1898. Launched from the yard of A & J Inglis, she was a handsome ship designed for North British express services to the coast resorts. She did not disappoint, attaining a speed of over 18 knots on her trials. Here she is seen off Gourock Pier en route for Craigendoran on 13 June 1935 while sailing in LNER colours. The new* **Marchioness of Lorne** *is off her port bow.*

The **Talisman** *(II), the first diesel–electric paddle vessel in the world, was built by A & J Inglis in 1935 for the LNER. She looked like a conventional Clyde steamer, even having proper paddle-boxes. Initially unreliable, she also had phenomenal levels of noise and vibration but a bonus was her economical running. This first-season photograph taken on 24 August 1935 near Kirn shows her with black bulwarks.*

Launched in 1936 by Wm Denny of Dumbarton for the CSP, the **Arran Mail** *was built to transport goods between Ardrossan and Arran. On 20 September 1938 she is seen alongside Burns Laird Lines'* **Lairdscrest** *at Ardrossan.*

The **Royal Scotsman** *was built by Harland & Wolff at Belfast and launched in March 1936. Here the brand–new ship, dressed overall, is seen at the Broomielaw two days before commencing her Belfast sailings on 15 June that year.*

*The **Lairdscastle** (I) was built in 1924 by the Ardrossan Dockyard Company and launched as the **Lady Limerick**. Transferred to Burns & Laird Lines in 1930 and having superior accommodation, she was placed on the Belfast night service from Glasgow. Outward bound, she is seen surging past the Custom House Quay at Greenock on 5 August 1939. She was lost by collision the following year.*

*In 1898 this ship came from A & J Inglis, entering service on the Londonderry route for G & J Burns as the **Magpie**. By 1929, she had been renamed the **Lairdsgrove**. Here as a passenger ship she arrives at Greenock, a calling point, on 17 July 1937.*

*The **Lairdsburn** (I), ex Lady Louth, was built by the Ardrossan Dockyard Company in 1923; this vessel was also placed on the Glasgow–Belfast night sailings. She is seen leaving Ardrossan on 17 July 1937.*

*Launched in 1902 as the **Rose** for the Glasgow, Dublin & Londonderry Steam Packet Company and the Laird Line, this ship had a reputation for stability on routes to Ireland. After employment as a troopship in the Mediterranean in the First World War, she resumed her Clyde sailings. In 1929 she was renamed the **Lairdsrose** and is seen passing the new **Renfrew Steam Ferry** (II) on her way down river on 22 July 1938.*

Built by Harland & Wolff at Belfast in 1936, the **Royal Ulsterman** *was a twin of* **Royal Scotsman***. Here the* **Royal Ulsterman** *lies at the Broomie[n] 19 May 1939 with the imposing Clyde Navigation Trust offices as a backdrop.*

The **Marchioness of Graham**, *built by Fairfields in 1936 – though smaller than the Duchesses – was a modern turbine steamer as this view taken at Ardrossan on 16 July 1937 shows. Placed on the demanding Ardrossan-Arran route, her promenade deck was designed for vehicle transport as car traffic to and from the island was increasing, but it could also accommodate penned livestock.*

The **Marchioness of Graham** *is also seen leaving Ardrossan in the company of the* **Glen Sannox** *on 16 July 1937, thereby revealing a contrast in styles.*

*The **Juno** (II) was launched from Fairfield's yard at Govan in 1937 for the CSP fleet and like her sister the **Jupiter** had space for cars between her funnels. Here the new **Juno** leaves astern from Wemyss Bay on a glassy sea on 2 August 1937. The Second World War saw the end of this fine steamer. While in process of conversion to an anti-aircraft vessel in the Thames in 1941, she was destroyed in the London Blitz.*

The Caledonia (II) was built by Wm Denny at Dumbarton and launched in 1934. As she was so different from the 'same name' steamer which she replaced, some adverse comments were made about her appearance – from the concealed paddle-boxes to the chunky profile. However, this **Caledonia** *proved versatile, serving on many routes and on excursions. She is seen here en route for Wemyss Bay on 26 June 1937.*

*The **Waverley** (III) is also seen coming into Rothesay Pier on 10 July 1937 when LNER vessels had grey hulls. There are child safety nets on her promenade deck.*

On 1 July 1937, the **Marmion** *is seen in Rothesay Bay, sporting the LNER's recently-adopted grey-hulled livery. During the latter 1930s, several steamer operators (most notably the Isle of Man Steam Packet Co.) switched from black hulls to schemes more akin to cruise vessels of the period, such as Cunard's first* **Mauretania**, *or the Blue Star liner* **Arandora Star**.

Summer and winter the **Talisman** *(II) sailed from Craigendoran to Rothesay and the Kyles of Bute, making calls at Port Bannatyne en route to Tighnabruaich. She is seen there on 1 July 1937 with the grey hull of a LNER vessel.*

On 8 July 1939 the **Waverley (III)** *was photographed laid up in Bowling Harbour with Scott of Bowling's* **Carola** *alongside. After the outbreak of the Second World War, the steamer was again requisitioned and gained lasting fame for the valour of her Captain and crew at the evacuation of Dunkirk. After heavy aerial attack, bravely repelled over many hours, the steamer sank in the English Channel. There is a commemorative plaque on board the present* **Waverley.**

On 10 August 1939, the **Marmion** *stirs up the waters at Dunoon. During the Second World War, she was again minesweeping and made three voyages to assist at Dunkirk. Sadly, the steamer was sunk by bombing at Harwich in 1941, and although salvaged was then scrapped.*

Off Kirn on 20 July 1936, the **Kenilworth** *has the grey LNER hull. She was withdrawn and broken up two years later.*

The **Jeanie Deans** (II) was one of the most popular steamers on the Clyde. 'The Jeanie', as she was affectionately known, came from Fairfield's yard at Govan in 1931. Based at Craigendoran, she was long and fast, attaining about 18 knots on her trials. After one season, the steamer reappeared with lengthened but oddly unequal funnels. She is seen arriving at Rothesay on 10 August 1939.

The **Talisman** is seen at Dunoon on 20 June 1939, photographed from **Queen Mary II**.

The **Lucy Ashton** also had the grey hull introduced on LNER steamers in 1936. In this guise, she comes into Princes Pier, Greenock, on 5 August 1939.

The **Jeanie Deans** *(II) leaving Dunoon on 10 August 1939.*

*By 20 June 1939 when viewed near Craigmore, the **Queen-Empress** was in CSP colours but was not in its actual ownership until 1943. On the outbreak of war that year, her minesweeping duties recommenced. After 1945, the **Queen-Empress** was not worth refitting, being sold three years later for scrapping.*

*The **Leven** was a small motor ship, which like her sister **Ashton**, was launched from Denny's yard at Dumbarton in 1938 for cruising in Glasgow Harbour. However, she was soon seen on the Gourock-Kilcreggan run and was a naval tender during the Second World War. In 1947, she was on the Largs-Millport route. Sold in 1965, she is now at Weston-super-Mare as the **Bristol Queen**.*

*The **Jupiter** (II) came from the Fairfield shipyard in 1937. Signs of the times were the enclosed paddle-boxes and the space between the funnels for carrying motor cars. The loading and unloading of vehicles by means of planks from the quayside was entertaining for onlookers but fraught for the vehicle owners. Here the **Jupiter** leaves Dunoon in some haste on 19 June 1939.*

*A view from 30 June 1939 sees the **King Edward** passing the Water's Neb with the Cunarder **Queen Elizabeth** in the fitting-out basin at John Brown's at Clydebank in the background.*

*Another pre-war view shows the **Jupiter** (II) coming alongside the Rothesay berth at Wemyss Bay.*

The MacBrayne screw steamer **Hebrides***, designed by the famous naval architect G. L. Watson, was built in 1898 and subsequently owned by McCallum, Orme & Co Ltd of Glasgow. She was primarily a cargo vessel serving remote places in the Western Isles but in summer ventured as far as St Kilda on popular tours from Glasgow and Greenock. When viewed passing Rothesay Dock on 30 June 1939, the* **Hebrides** *was sailing on such cruises. She was withdrawn in 1955.*

MacBrayne's **Lochiel** *came from Wm Denny at Dumbarton in 1939. Although similar in appearance to the* **Lochnevis***, her motor propulsion was improved and almost vibration-free. Here the new ship is at Fort William on 30 August 1939. However, it was the West Loch Tarbert–Islay run where the* **Lochiel** *became best known, sailing there for thirty years.*

During the Second World War, the **Duchess of Argyll** served both as a ferry on various Clyde routes and as a tender to troopships. Here she is seen at Kilmun in 1946 in war grey, and looking much neglected.

In the Second World War, the **Duchess of Montrose** was on the Wemyss Bay-Rothesay route. On 4 June 1946, the war-weary ship was photographed coming into Wemyss Bay Pier.

On the outbreak of the Second World War in 1939, the **Eagle III** again became a minesweeper, named HMS **Oriole**, and was also at Dunkirk. When the hostilities were over, she was laid up in the Holy Loch and in 1946 was sold for scrapping at Smith & Houston's yard at Port Glasgow.

The **Jeanie Deans** *survived the Second World War, returning to the Clyde for a radical reconstruction. This involved deck shelters, modern davits, new funnels (this time of equal height) and a mainmast. Her accommodation improvements made her passenger facilities 'up market'. These views were taken off Kirn in September 1946 (top) and Rothesay in June 1946 (right) and June 1947 (left).*

After wartime adventures, the Talisman came back to the Clyde where she re-appeared in LNER colours, and is viewed off Innellan on 21 June 1947.

By 1947, the Lucy Ashton was back into her peacetime routine and is seen leaving Gourock for Craigendoran on 10 June with her bridge now enclosed.

*The **Waverley** (IV) first entered the LNER fleet and makes a stirring sight arriving at Rothesay on 21 June 1947. Her traditional paddle-boxes were much admired.*

*The **Waverley** (IV) has the distinction of being the last of the Clyde steamers. Launched from the yard of A & J Inglis at Pointhouse on 2 October 1946, the vessel was dressed overall and the expectation was that she would be the first of several new paddle steamers.*

On the outbreak of the Second World War, when all the LNER ships had left, the **Lucy Ashton** continued sailings from Craigendoran to the inner Firth piers and in 1945 to Innellan and Rothesay. Through the war years she was only off one week – a sterling effort by such an elderly vessel. The steamer is seen here in British Transport Commission livery in 1947.

Throughout the Second World War, the little **Ashton** and **Leven** were tenders on the Firth. Post-1945, they ran a summer service from Gourock to Dunoon. This view of the **Ashton** was taken in 1949. After use as the Millport ferry, in 1965 she was purchased for the Gourock-Helensburgh route and renamed the **Gourockian**. She later went to England becoming the **Wyre Lady**.

In 1947, the **Lucy Ashton** attained sixty years' service, marked by a special cruise on 19 May for the Clyde River Steamer Club. She is seen at Rothesay on that occasion.

In 1947, the **Waverley** *came into the ownership of the British Transport Commission, and is in BR colours when seen off Craigendoran on 29 May 1948. She was frequently used on Rothesay, Kyles of Bute and 'Round Bute' cruises.*

The **Duchess of Hamilton** *(II) was almost identical to the* **Duchess of Montrose** *but came from the Govan yard of Harland & Wolff Ltd in 1932. Here in Rothesay Bay on 29 May 1948 the* **Duchess of Hamilton** *is dressed overall when on a private charter to ICI (Imperial Chemical Industries). The naval vessel in the background is a submarine depot ship.*

*Post-war, the **Duchess of Argyll** was again on Kyles of Bute runs and was photographed approaching Gourock on 17 June 1946. In 1952 the steamer was sold for experimental purposes to the Admiralty and was scrapped in 1970.*

In BR control and colours, the **Jeanie Deans** *sails from Gourock on 19 September 1951. In 1963, the steamer was sold to a group of paddle steamer enthusiasts in London. Renamed the* **Queen of the South** *and with her funnels again in LNER colours, she began cruises on the Thames. Sadly, breakdowns required further expenditure but disappointments continued and in 1967 she was sold to shipbreakers in Belgium.*

The **Talisman** *is seen in British Railways' livery leaving Gourock on 29 May 1949. Re-engined in 1954 she took up the Millport run. Withdrawn in 1966, she was broken up at Dalmuir the following year.*

One of Ernest's first colour slides taken with a miniature camera shows MacBrayne's motor vessel **Lochearn** *tied up at Oban Railway Pier on 19 May 1951 during the company's Centenary Year.*

The handsome MacBrayne steamer **Lochness** *glides past the Hutcheson Monument on Kerrera on her way into Oban Bay on 19 May 1951.*

In morning light the **King George V** *leaves from the Railway Pier at Oban on 30 May 1953 at the beginning of another cruise to Iona.*

A deck scene on the **King George V,** *which with her red funnels and varnished deckhouses formed a traditional setting for passengers dressed in the typical outdoor wear of the 1950s — mainly tweeds and waterproofs.*

The view aft on the **King George V** *as she sails away from Staffa after landing passengers there on 23 June 1959.*

The **King George V** *then swings past the Town Pier at Oban. Always immaculately turned out, the 1926-vintage steamer continued in service until the end of the 1974 season by which time she was the oldest ship in the combined Caledonian MacBrayne fleet.*

The King George V *lies at anchor in the Sound of Iona on 30 June 1959 while visitors stroll on the jetty amid goods conveyed by the steamer.*

Surrounded by pink sand and tranquil turquoise water, the **King George V** *arrives at Iona on 2 June 1953 – Coronation Day. To mark the occasion, the steamer is dressed overall.*

Before the car ferry era, the transport of motor vehicles was a challenge for MacBrayne crews. At Oban on 14 May 1960 the Lochinvar displays a range of cargo including mailbags and laundry baskets plus cars of British manufacture.

Under a damp grey sky and with her silhouette reflected in still water, the **Duchess of Hamilton** *lies at Campbeltown Pier on 12 June 1951.*

Viewed from Cardwell Bay and silhouetted against an unsettled sky, the CSP near-sisters **Duchess of Hamilton** *and* **Duchess of Montrose** *are moored at Gourock's Railway Pier. This was the company's headquarters established by the Caledonian Railway in 1889 and now continues as the base for Caledonian MacBrayne.*

The Caledonian Steam Packet (British Railways) paddle steamer **Jupiter** *gathers speed and heads across the Firth towards Dunoon on 12 June 1953.*

The SS Ardyne off Gourock on 12 June 1953. Built at Bowling in 1928 for Clyde Cargo Steamers Ltd, she carried general cargo to Campbeltown and later to Arran. Better road transport and the advent of car ferries brought her career to an end in 1955, when she was broken up at Troon.

The paddle steamer **Caledonia** leaves Gourock Pier on 19 September 1951. One of a series of similar vessels introduced in the 1930s to replace Edwardian-era tonnage, the **Caledonia**, in common with her half-sisters, had disguised paddle-boxes, perhaps better to resemble the CSP's turbine steamers.

In late-summer sunshine, the **Queen Mary II** approaches Gourock Pier on 19 September 1951 en route from Bridge Wharf on her daily sailing to Rothesay and Tighnabruaich.

Then off Gourock, the **Queen Mary II** is seen on passage to Dunoon that day. Later, in the mid-1950s, the steamer was reboilered and fitted with a single large funnel.

The hilly slopes of the Firth of Clyde make an attractive background as the paddle steamer **Marchioness of Lorne** *approaches Gourock from Dunoon on 19 September 1951.*

The unique diesel-electric Clyde paddle steamer **Talisman** *is seen off Gourock making for Craigendoran on 12 September 1952 during a NATO Fleet Review.*

The versatile paddle steamer **Jupiter** *approaches Gourock Pier from Dunoon on 12 June 1953.*

At the end of her lengthy career, the withdrawn paddle steamer **Duchess of Fife** *lies forlornly in the Albert Harbour at Greenock on the evening of 12 June 1953. The veteran steamer was a Clyde favourite, hence this special trip to photograph the last of the old 'Caley' fleet before she was consigned for scrapping.*

The recently-delivered **Maid of Ashton** *makes for Gourock Pier on 12 June 1953. Delivered from the Clyde yard of Yarrows, best known as a builder of naval vessels, the 627-passenger motor ship had a hull form somewhat reminiscent of a minesweeper.*

The new motor ship **Maid of Argyll** *leaves Gourock on 12 June 1953. One of four practically identical sisters, the 'Maids' were the final class of Clyde passenger ships delivered before the advent of the car ferry era.*

The Queen Mary II *moves away from the Bridge Wharf. The* Lairds Ben *and the* Irish Coast *can be discerned. The steamer is well loaded with passengers bound for the Clyde resorts – note the pram complete with canopy on the aft deck. The date is 26 June 1953.*

The **Lairds Loch** *was built by the Ardrossan Dockyard Company and delivered in 1944 as an austerity cargo steamer, later being converted to carry passengers. During the 1950s and early 1960s, she served on the Glasgow-Londonderry route, being sold in 1966 to Israeli interests. The Sailors' Home, with its distinctive tower, is seen in this view near the Broomielaw.*

On 26 June 1953, the Burns & Laird motor ship **Royal Ulsterman** *is at the Broomielaw between her overnight sailings to Belfast.*

The **Irish Coast** *passes the entrance to Queen's Dock and the crossing point for the Kelvinhaugh Ferry as she progresses down river at the commencement of her evening sailing from Glasgow to Dublin on 12 June 1953.*

The **Irish Coast** *heads down the Clyde, passing Govan Dry Dock on her way to Dublin on the evening of 12 June 1953. Built by Harland &*
Wolff in Belfast and delivered that year, the **Irish Coast** *sailed under charter to Burns & Laird.*

The most impressive steamer on the Firth of Clyde was MacBrayne's three-funnelled **Saint Columba**, *seen leaving Gourock on 12 June 1953. This ship was the result of a radical transformation in 1936 of the* **Queen Alexandra (II)** *of 1912 and was placed on the prestigious Glasgow–Ardrishaig route.*

Left, the **Saint Columba** *approaches Gourock for Greenock on the same day.*

Viewed from Greenock Esplanade, MacBrayne's **Saint Columba** *steams up river en route from Ardrishaig to Glasgow, while Cunard's recently-delivered liner* **Carinthia** *lies at anchor at the Tail of the Bank on the evening of 15 June 1956.*

MacBrayne's classic motor ship **Lochfyne** *leaves Rothesay on 15 April 1954. Re-engined the previous year, the* **Lochfyne** *continued on the Clyde, latterly operating on the Ardrishaig mail run until 1969.*

The elegant turbine steamer **Duchess of Hamilton** *departs from Rothesay on 11 September 1954. This vessel and her near sister, the* **Duchess of Montrose,** *were favourites of Ernest.*

A close-up study shows the CSP turbine steamer **Marchioness of Graham** *approaching Gourock Pier on the afternoon of 16 April 1954. Long associated with the Arran run, the 1936-vintage steamer continued in the CSP fleet until 1958 when, having been replaced by car ferries, she was sold to Greek interests.*

On 11 September 1954, the majestic Canadian Pacific trans-Atlantic liner **Empress of Scotland** lies at the Tail of the Bank with the PS **Waverley** tied up against her starboard side, acting as tender for Canada-bound passengers from the Clyde. The CSP fleet frequently tendered to the great Cunard and CP liners when they called, en route from Liverpool to Montreal.

The second of the CSP's 'first generation' of so-called 'ABC' car ferries, the Cowal, speeds past Kirn on 16 April 1954. Recently delivered from Ailsa Shipbuilding, the side-loading ferry began her career on the Gourock-Dunoon crossing, before switching in October 1954 to inaugurate the Wemyss Bay-Rothesay car ferry service.

The CSP car ferry Cowal uses her vehicle hoist at Gourock. At low tide, a trolley loaded with mailbags and milk churns is offloaded, with two vans waiting to follow on 16 April 1954. Next, an Armstrong Siddeley Sapphire, followed by Ford and Morris vans, prepares to drive off the Cowal's vehicle lift at Gourock. Note that the deck crew are wearing BR (British Railways Shipping) jerseys.

Built in 1908, the **Vehicular Ferry No 3** *had a hoistable vehicle deck, capable of maintaining a constant height relative to the quays in Glasgow Harbour at any state of the tide. Here, she is seen at Finnieston carrying an interesting collection of lorries – including an Albion and a Foden. The notorious Betty's Bar occupies the ground floor of the tenement in the background. The ferry was scrapped in 1966.*

On 10 September 1956, the chain-driven ferry at Erskine, named appropriately **Erskine** – which dated from 1936 and, as the **Renfrew**, had initially operated up river between Renfrew and Yoker – clanks across the Clyde, her vehicle deck containing a fine collection of period cars.

The **Erskine** offloads at Erskine Jetty. Amongst the cars coming ashore are Austins - a Cambridge being followed by an A40 Somerset. The **Erskine** was laid up after the crossing was replaced by a bridge in June 1971. Eventually she fell derelict and sank in the Clyde at the Pudzeoch Basin, finally being broken up where she lay.

On the evening of 16 April 1954, the veteran steamers **Lairds Isle**, **Ardyne** *and* **Glen Sannox** *lie in the Albert Harbour at Greenock.*
Although the **Lairds Isle** *enjoyed four more seasons ferrying passengers between Ardrossan and Belfast, the* **Glen Sannox** *was sold for scrap to Belgian shipbreakers only a couple of months after this image was taken.*

97

A stern-quarter shot shows Coast Lines' attractive motor ship Irish Coast, berthed at Lancefield Quay on the sunny morning of 2 June 1955. Later that evening, she would set sail for Dublin.

On 2 June 1955, the Burns & Laird steamer Lairdshill was moored at Merklands Wharf. Built in 1921 at Ardrossan as the Ardmore for the Glasgow–Dublin route, she had subsequently served B&I during the mid-1930s as the Lady Longford before moving back to Glasgow. Latterly associated with the Londonderry service, she was scrapped at Dublin in 1957.

Under a cloud of dense smoke and steam, the veteran Burns & Laird Ardrossan-Belfast steamer **Lairds Isle** manoeuvres in Ardrossan Harbour on 10 September 1956. Completed in 1911 as the **Riviera** for the South Eastern & Chatham Railway's Dover-Calais service, the vessel was acquired by Burns & Laird in 1932.

The graceful **Lairds Isle** is alongside Winton Pier at Ardrossan before setting off on her regular daytime crossing to Belfast on 10 September 1956. Her counter stern and lofty funnels were a reminder of the elegance of Channel steamers of the Edwardian era.

With her funnels belching smoke, the **Lairds Isle** sets sail for Belfast on 10 September 1956.

(Inset) By the latter 1960s, the once extensive Burns & Laird and Coast Lines network of Irish Sea routes had been greatly reduced and much of the old fleet withdrawn. In December 1967, a new car ferry for the Ardrossan–Belfast route, named the **Lion**, was delivered by Cammell Laird of Birkenhead. Seen here at Ardrossan in 1972, she was initially a success but, by the mid-1970s, political violence in Northern Ireland had reduced the number of passengers on the route and the **Lion** was redeployed on the Dover Strait.

The **Jeanie Deans** *is seen off Gourock in the early 1960s. By this stage, the double gold strakes on her hull had been painted out and the deckhouses were white painted rather than finished in wood grain-effect varnish.*

The car ferry **Arran** *leaves Gourock on 15 June 1956. One of a class of three delivered to the CSP in 1953-54, the* **Arran** *loaded cars and small trucks via ingenious side-ramps which doubled as lifts to enable use at all states of the tide. The process was relatively slow and tortuous, however, and so by the 1970s ferry linkspans were installed at the key Clyde steamer piers.*

A selection of 1950s cars signals the advent of the new order at the former Glasgow & South Western terminus at Princes Pier, Greenock, in the summer of 1957. The **Jupiter** *rests between sailings to and from Dunoon, while the funnel of a Ross & Marshall puffer can be seen in the background. Today, the site is occupied by Clydeport's container and cruise terminal.*

The **Maid of Ashton** *cruises towards Gourock Pier on a 1959
summer's afternoon. The vessel continued in the CSP fleet until
1971 when her rail-connected ferrying of passengers across the
Clyde from ports such as Craigendoran and Gourock was
superseded by car ferry traffic.*

Dramatic evening sunlight catches the **Maid of Cumbrae** *off Gourock in June 1956. Thr four 'Maids' were popular on shorter crossings of the Firth of Clyde until displaced by car ferries in the early 1970s.*

Aboard the **Waverley** *in 1962, two passengers pose with the Assistant Purser, Leslie Brown. For student steamer enthusiasts, this job had numerous attractions, including wearing a CSP officer's uniform. Leslie is, of course, well known today for his sterling efforts to ensure the conservation and continued operation of the* **Waverley** *and for his hard work to raise funds to return the* **Maid of the Loch** *to active service on Loch Lomond.*

The 1957-built Arran car ferry **Glen Sannox** *calls at Brodick Pier during the early summer of 1959, while the Hay-owned 'puffer'* **Boer** *goes astern nearby. As with the existing 'ABC' ferries, the* **Glen Sannox** *had a crane mounted on her stern, but this was subsequently removed and a stern car ramp was installed in its place during a substantial 1971-72 winter refit.*

A deck scene on the Arran car ferry **Glen Sannox** *in fine summer weather in 1959.*

*Seen here in 1959 at Brodick Pier with Goat Fell in the background, the car ferry **Glen Sannox** was a Clyde favourite for many years. Built in Troon for the Arran route, she continued in Scottish waters until 1989 when she was sold for Red Sea service between Egypt and Saudi Arabia. Remarkably, she survives as an abandoned hulk, grounded on a reef off Jeddah.*

The Lochfyne awaits her passengers at Gourock Pier in 1959 with one of the CSP's 'ABC' ferries berthed astern. By this stage, the Lochfyne had replaced the turbine steamer Saint Columba on the Ardrishaig run. The installations abaft the bridge did not enhance the ship's profile.

In June 1959 Oban Bay shelters the Claymore *and the* Lochinvar *alongside the Railway Pier while a lighthouse tender (left) and a collier (right) are also in view.*

Between downpours, a shaft of sunlight brightens the MacBrayne's motor vessels **Claymore** *and* **Lochmor***, berthed together at Lochboisdale in the early 1960s.*

MacBrayne's **Claymore** *lies at the Railway Pier at Oban on 30 June 1959. Built by Wm Denny at Dumbarton and delivered in 1955, this popular ship served Coll, Tiree, Castlebay and Lochboisdale until the early 1970s. She was sold to Greece in 1976.*

*A mid-1960s view of MacBrayne's car ferry **Hebrides** (II) at Tarbert, Harris. The **Hebrides** was one of three near-identical sisters built by Hall, Russell in Aberdeen to serve on routes from Oban. Sold in 1986 for use as the **Devoniun** sailing from Torquay to the Channel Islands, she passed to Albanian interests in 1993 becoming the **Illyria**. A serious engine room fire ended her career in 1999 and she was scrapped in 2003.*

The car ferry Caledonia *was a controversial second-hand addition to the CSP fleet. Built in Norway in 1966 as the Swedish-owned* Stena Baltica, *she was rebuilt for the Ardrossan-Brodick service in 1970. Unfortunately, she proved to be an unpredictable performer in the challenging waters of the Firth of Clyde. She is seen here at Ardrossan in June 1972.*

The ferry **Caledonia** *arrives at Ardrossan from Brodick in 1971. While this vessel introduced drive-through operation, she was unable to maintain her schedule in rough weather. She was quickly moved to the more sheltered Oban-Craignure (Mull) route on which she plied until 1987.*

Newly-converted to a stern- and side-loading car ferry of sorts, the **Maid of Cumbrae** *sets off from Gourock Pier in 1972. Only five years later, she was replaced by the much larger* **Saturn** *and, thereafter, sold for further service in the Bay of Naples. Finally, she was scrapped in Turkey in 2006.*

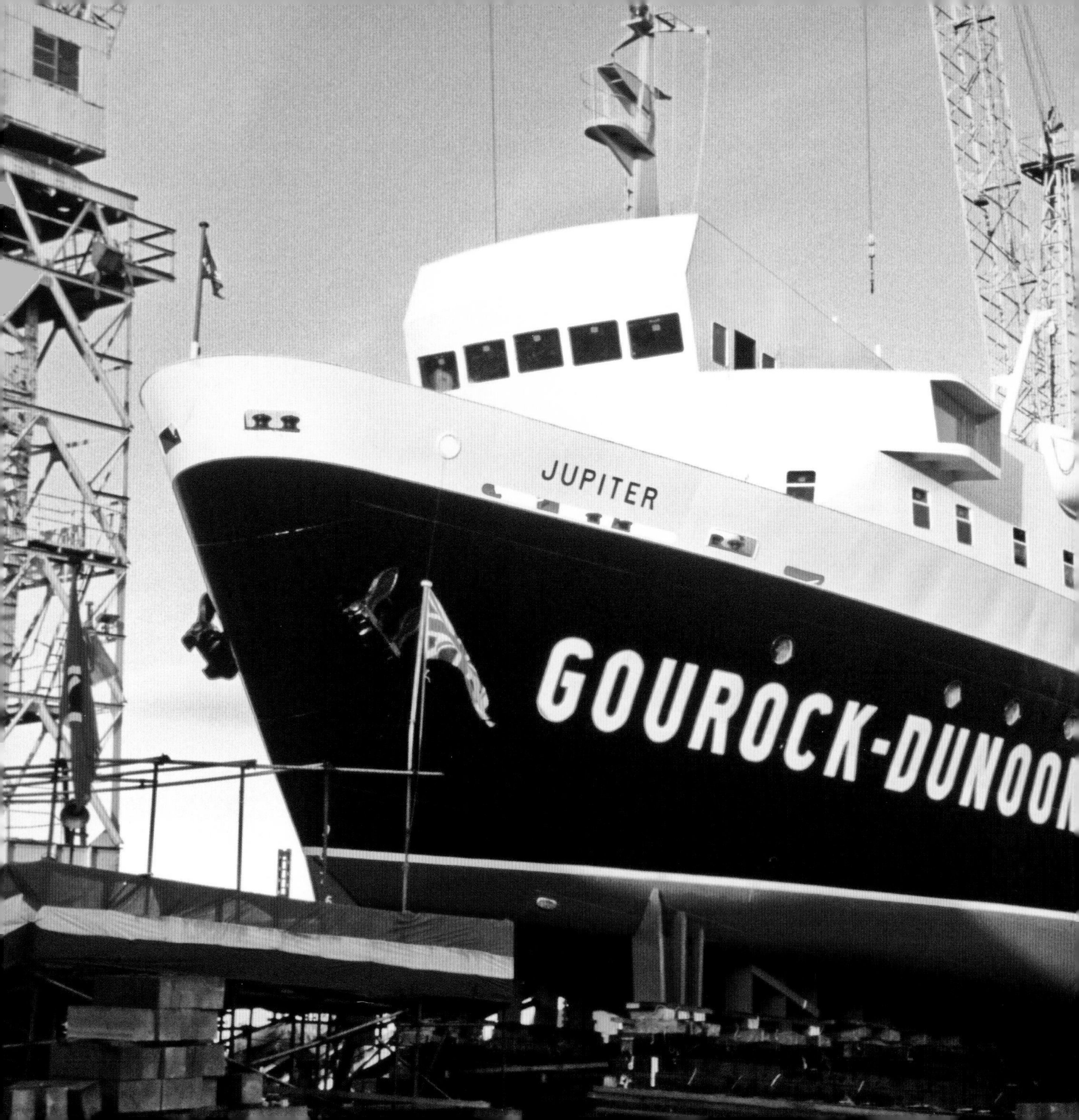
JUPITER
GOUROCK-DUNOON

On the bright morning of 27 November 1973, the Caledonian MacBrayne car ferry **Jupiter (III)** is prepared for launching at James Lamont's Port Glasgow shipyard. This highly versatile Voith–Schneider-propelled vessel continues to serve the CalMac fleet in 2009.

(Inset) On 27 November 1973 preparatory to fitting out in the Albert Harbour at Greenock, the newly-launched **Jupiter** has the Cory tug **Vanguard** alongside. In the background, the **Maid of Argyll** and the **Queen Mary** are in CalMac livery, but the withdrawn **Duchess of Hamilton** remains in CSP colours. Truly, this was the 'changing of the guard'- from the steamer era to that of the car ferries.

A mid-1970s view of Gourock Pier with the excursion vessel **Keppel** in the foreground and **Queen Mary**, *by then the last remaining Clyde turbine steamer, in the middle-distance. (Her name had shed 'II' in 1967 when the Cunard liner was withdrawn). The Keppel had been built in 1961 as the* **Rose**, *one of three sisters for British Rail's Tilbury-Gravesend ferry across the Thames Estuary. Acquired by the CSP for Clyde operation in 1967, she continued until 1992 when sold to Maltese owners.*

Ernest Glen's ship photography covered paddle steamers of the 1900s to the modern 'double-decker' car and freight ferries of the 1980s. Here, British Rail Sealink's brand-new Harland & Wolff-built **Galloway Princess** *is undergoing trials on the Firth of Clyde on 9 March 1980.*

The view aft from the port bridge wing as the **Duchess of Hamilton** *sails on the Firth of Clyde in late afternoon sunlight on 12 June 1951. Ernest was regularly welcomed on steamer bridges but preferred to roam the decks meeting friends and taking photographs.*

Above: This prospect of Gourock from the Lyle Hill on 16 April 1954 shows an impressive lineup at the Railway Pier - (from left to right) the **Waverley** is followed by the **Marchioness of Graham**, the **Arran**, the **Maid of Ashton** and the **Cowal**. At anchor is the new tanker **Pacific Star** undergoing trials while two Admiralty tugs are moored at the jetty in Cardwell Bay.

Acknowledgements: The authors wish to express their thanks to Miles Cowsill and John Hendy of Ferry Publications for their enthusiastic support for this project, to John Peter for preparing the photographs, to David Parsons for copy-editing the manuscript, and to Iain Quinn, Ian Somerville and Ian Hall for their advice and information about Clyde steamers and piers.